DISCOVER!

PEOPLE of the PAST

WHO WAS ABIGAIL ADAMS?

Robert Clore

Enslow PUBLISHING

Please visit our website, www.enslow.com. For a free color catalog of all our high-quality books, call toll free 1-800-398-2504 or fax 1-877-980-4454.

Cataloging-in-Publication Data
Names: Clore, Robert.
Title: Who was Abigail Adams? / Robert Clore.
Description: Buffalo, NY : Enslow Publishing, 2027. | Series: People of the past | Includes glossary.
Identifiers: ISBN 9781978550414 (pbk.) | ISBN 9781978550421 (library bound) | ISBN 9781978550438 (ebook)
Subjects: LCSH: Adams, Abigail, 1744-1818–Juvenile literature. | Presidents' spouses–United States–Biography–Juvenile literature. | United States–History–Revolution, 1775-1783–Juvenile literature.
Classification: LCC E322.1.A38 C657 2027 | DDC 973.44092 B–dc23

Published in 2027 by
Enslow Publishing
2544 Clinton Street
Buffalo, NY 14224

Designer: Claire Vanden Branden
Editor: Max Pritchard

Photo Credits: Cover, pp. 1, 7, 9, 21 Everett Collection/Shutterstock.com; pp. 5, 17 Library of Congress; p. 11 Enrico Della Pietra/Shutterstock.com; pp. 13, 19 Wikimedia Commons; p. 15 Rawpixel.com/Shutterstock.com.

Printed in China

CPSIA compliance information: Batch #QS27ENS: For further information contact Enslow Publishing, at 1-800-398-2504.

CONTENTS

BOLDFACE WORDS APPEAR IN THE GLOSSARY.

A LADY OF LETTERS

Abigail Adams was a famous woman. She was one of the most well-known women of the late 1700s and early 1800s. She was very interested in **politics**. She helped shape the early history of the United States. She wrote many letters that show people today what life was like when the United States was founded.

CHILDHOOD

Abigail was born in Massachusetts in 1744. Abigail lived with her parents, brother, and three sisters. She was often sick. And most schools only taught boys. So Abigail learned at home. She read a lot.

BOSTON, MASSACHUSETTS, WAS AN IMPORTANT CITY IN THE 1700s.

MR. AND MRS. ADAMS

Abigail met John Adams in 1762. He was a lawyer. Abigail and John married in 1764. John cared a lot about politics too. Abigail and John wanted the **colonies** to be **independent** from Great Britain. In 1774, John went to Philadelphia to help form a new government.

JOHN ADAMS

Abigail stayed at their home in Massachusetts. She raised their five children and ran their farm. Abigail and John wrote each other letters while he was gone. She told him to support women's rights. She believed strongly in women's right to education.

THE ADAMS HOME AT ADAMS NATIONAL HISTORICAL PARK

A SEA APART

The **American Revolution** ended with victory for the colonies. Afterwards, John went to France and Britain to represent the United States. Abigail continued to write letters to him. She told him how the new government was doing while he was away.

ADAMS, LOWER LEFT,
WITH OTHER
US REPRESENTATIVES

GOVERNMENT DUTIES

In 1789, George Washington chose John as his vice president. Abigail became Second Lady. "Second Lady" means wife of the vice president. John was vice president for eight years. Abigail traveled between their home in Massachusetts and the nation's capital during that time.

GEORGE WASHINGTON

John became the nation's second president in 1797. Abigail became First Lady of the United States. John and Abigail were the first president and First Lady to live in the White House in Washington, DC. Abigail hosted guests and events there.

AN 1800s SKETCH OF THE WHITE HOUSE

Abigail often told John what she thought of government issues. John asked for her opinions on big problems. However, some people didn't think it was the First Lady's place to talk about politics. That didn't stop Abigail. She continued to speak her mind.

AFTER THE PRESIDENCY

John lost his second **election** in 1800. Abigail and John moved back to Massachusetts. Abigail taught her son, John Quincy. He became the sixth president. Abigail wrote many letters to family and friends during the rest of her life. After Abigail died in 1818, her letters became an important part of history.

JOHN QUINCY ADAMS

GLOSSARY

American Revolution: The war in which American colonists overthrew British control in order to choose a government run by the people.

colonies: Places that are under the control of another country.

election: The act of voting someone into a government position.

independent: Free, not ruled by something else.

politics: The activities of the government and government officials.

FOR MORE INFORMATION

Books

Murray, Stuart. *American Revolution*. New York, NY: DK Publishing, 2022.

Youssef, Jagger. *The Words of Abigail Adams*. New York, NY: PowerKids Press, 2023.

Websites

Britannica Kids: Abigail Adams
kids.britannica.com/kids/article/Abigail-Adams/399918
Read about Abigail's life and view photos of the Adams' family house and a coin celebrating Abigail.

First Ladies
firstladies.org/home/first-ladies
Learn about every woman to have held the role of First Lady.

INDEX